This book belongs to

Sleep

Bedtime is here and it's time to sleep.

Have you ever wondered who and what else sleeps?

Let's explore and see if the rest of nature sleeps too.

Koala Bears sleep a lot.

They sleep between 20-22 hours a day.
That's almost the whole day!

Horses can sleep standing up.

So can elephants and giraffes.

Ducks sleep with one eye open..

...and so do dolphins.

Otters hold hands while they sleep..

..so that they don't drift away while snoozing.

Octopuses can change colors while they are asleep. Wow!

Bats hang upside down while catching their z's.

Big dogs dream longer than little dogs.
Little dogs dream quickly and more often.

Cats sleep mostly during the daytime and even more when it's rainy or cold.

How do we know when insects are sleeping?

They stop moving, and some fold in their antennae.

A caterpillar sleeps 10 to 14 days in its chrysalis until it emerges as an adult butterfly.

Even trees and plants droop their branches at night and some close their leaves.

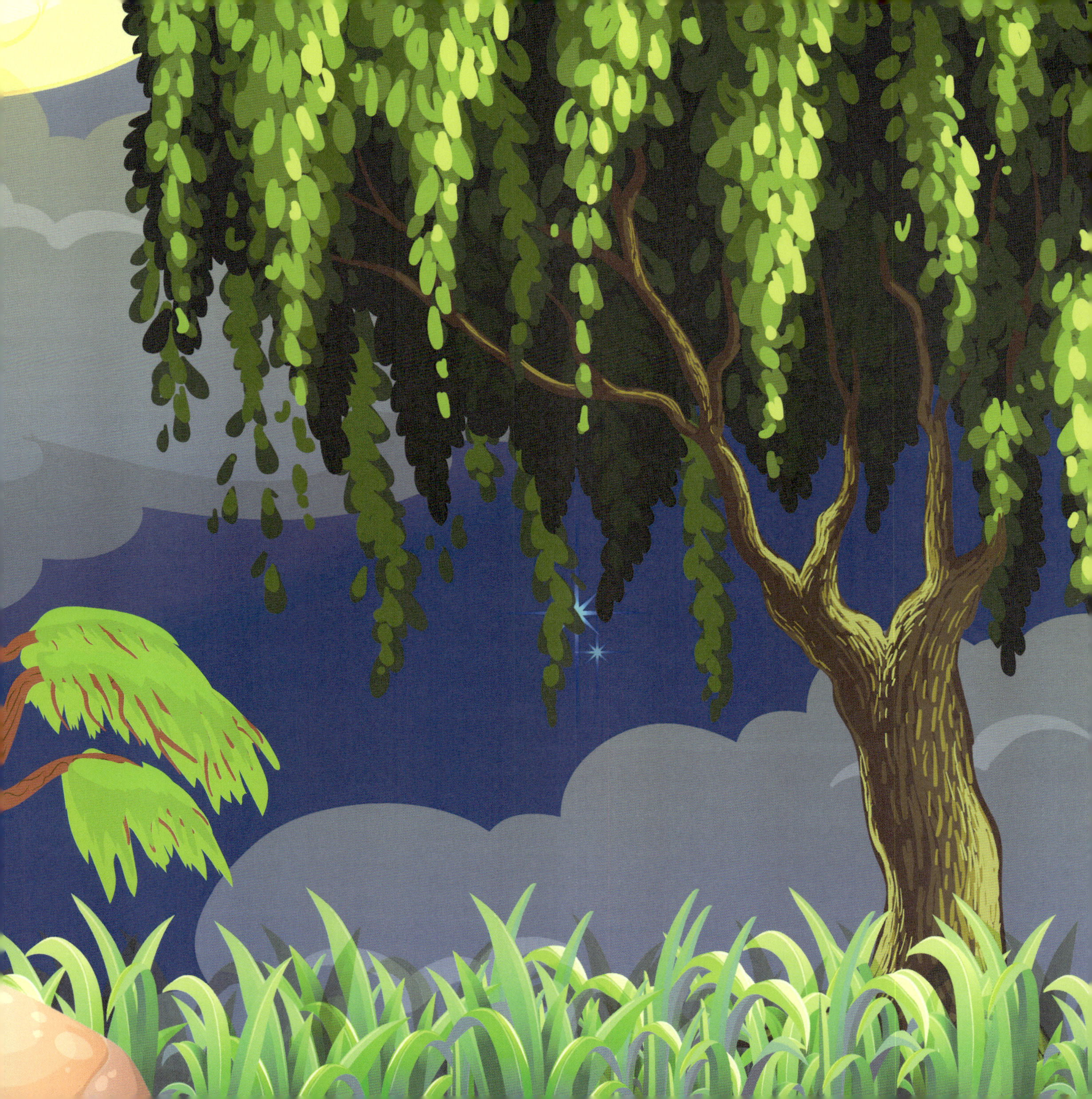

But only humans sleep with blankets, pillows, pj's and teddies!

And only humans get to read bedtime stories!

Good Night

Sweet Dreams

Copyright © 2021 by Sandy Ascenzi

Printed in Great Britain
by Amazon